A Simple-Machine Scavenger Hunt

by Jenna Lee Gleisner

The Child's World®
childsworld.com

Published by The Child's World®
1980 Lookout Drive • Mankato, MN 56003-1705
800-599-READ • www.childsworld.com

Photographs ©: Somchai Som/Shutterstock Images, cover (lightbulb), 3 (lightbulb), 11 (bottom center); Shutterstock Images, cover (top right), cover (bottom left), cover (bottom right), cover (screws), 3 (top left), 3 (bottom left), 3 (bottom right), 3 (screws), 3 (hammer), 4, 5 (top left), 5 (bottom left), 5 (bottom right), 8, 9 (top left), 9 (top right), 9 (bottom left), 9 (bottom right), 10, 11 (bottom right), 18, 19 (top left), 19 (top right), 19 (bottom left), 19 (bottom right), 21; Vladyslav Starozhylov/Shutterstock Images, cover (top left), 3 (top right), 11 (top); Gubin Yury/Shutterstock Images, 5 (top right); iStockphoto, 6, 13, 14; Gray Wall Studio/Shutterstock Images, 7; Tatiana Popova/Shutterstock Images, 11 (bottom left); Dmitry Tsvetkov/Shutterstock Images, 12; Elizaveta Galitckaia/Shutterstock Images, 15; Olesia Bilkei/Shutterstock Images, 16; Manuel Trinidad Mesa/Shutterstock Images, 17; Patrick Foto/Shutterstock Images, 20

Design Elements ©: Shutterstock Images; Somchai Som/Shutterstock Images; Vladyslav Starozhylov/Shutterstock Images

ISBN 9781503823679
LCCN 2017944885

Printed in the United States of America
PA02361

About the Author

Jenna Lee Gleisner is an author and editor who lives in Minnesota. She has written more than 80 books for children. When not writing or editing, she enjoys spending time with her family and her dog, Norrie.

Simple machines are everywhere! There are six types of simple machines. They help us do work. Turn the page and see if you can find the simple machines in this book!

3

An inclined plane is a flat surface that is slanted. One end is higher than the other. Things can easily go from a lower point to a higher point.

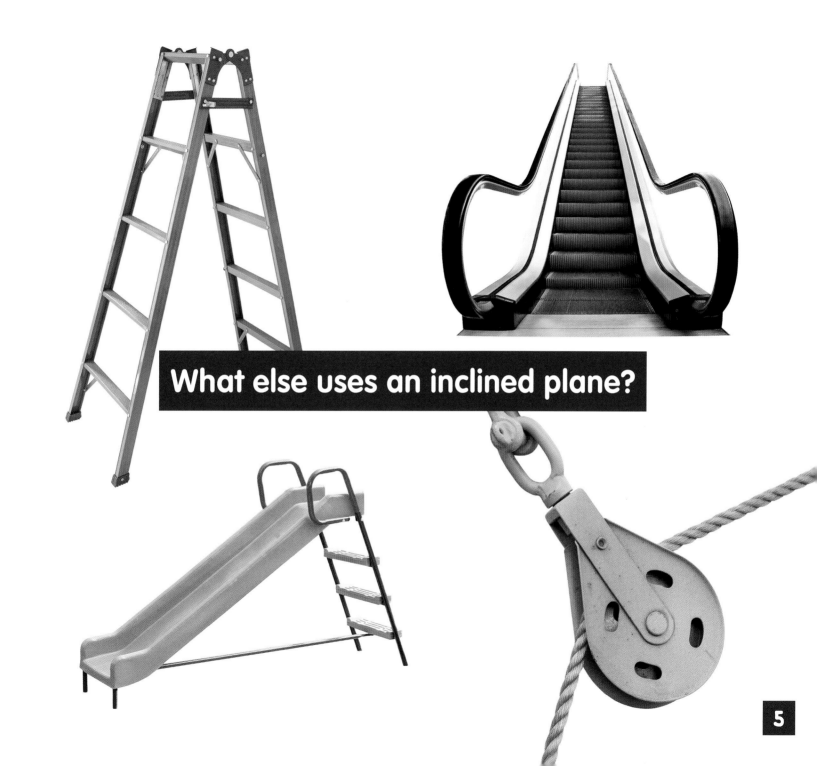

What else uses an inclined plane?

5

Gravity helps us move things from the higher to the lower point on an inclined plane. This worker wheels a cart of heavy boxes down an inclined plane.

How many inclined planes can you find at this water park?

A **wedge** is a type of inclined plane. It has at least one side that is slanted. It is used to separate objects. An axe wedges into wood and splits it. Wedges can also hold objects together. A doorstop wedges under a door. It keeps the door in place.

Which of these items are wedges?

A **screw** is a twisted inclined plane. It moves in a **circular** motion. A jar lid is an example of a screw.

What other objects are screws?

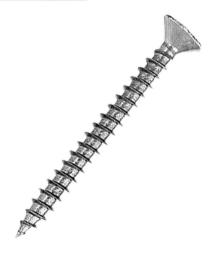

Wheels and axles work together. They help us move objects across distances. An axle is a rod in the middle of a wheel. The wheel turns around the axle. The axle helps the wheel spin in a circle. A pizza cutter is an example of a wheel and axle.

What kinds of wheels and axles
do you see in this picture?

13

A **pulley** is similar to a wheel and axle. But it has a rope or cord attached to pull things. Pulleys change the direction of **force**. If you pull down on the rope, the object moves up. Workers use pulleys to lift loads.

What pulleys do you see at work in this picture?

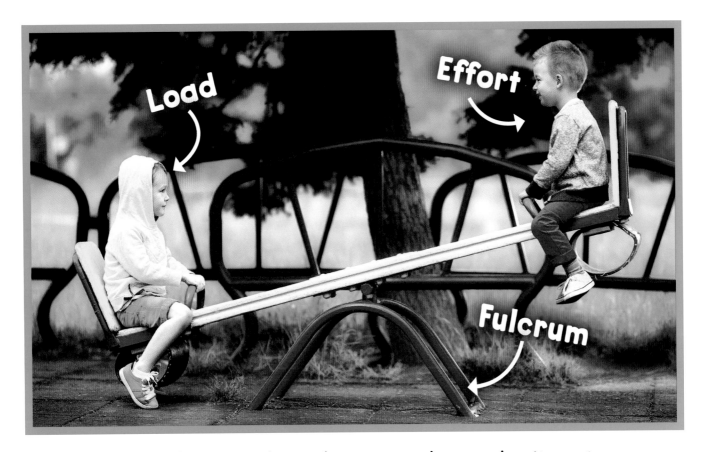

A lever is a long tool, such as a rod or pole. It rests on a fulcrum. A lever is placed under an object, or a load. Then force is used. The force applied to move the load is called effort. The lever pushes down against the fulcrum. The lever lifts the load.

Can you identify the lever and fulcrum in this picture?

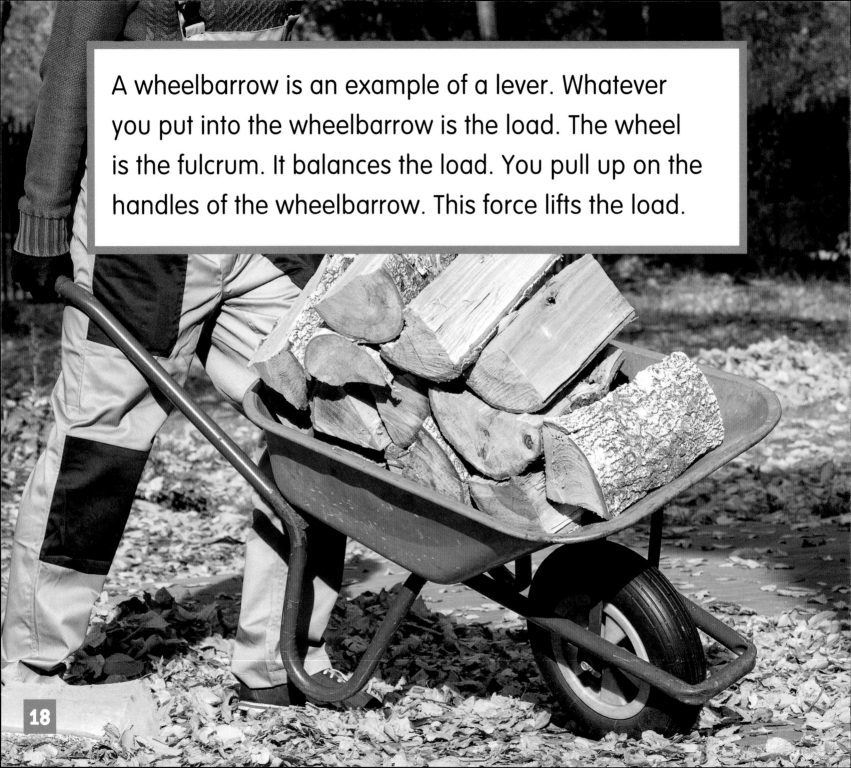

A wheelbarrow is an example of a lever. Whatever you put into the wheelbarrow is the load. The wheel is the fulcrum. It balances the load. You pull up on the handles of the wheelbarrow. This force lifts the load.

Which of these gardening tools are levers?

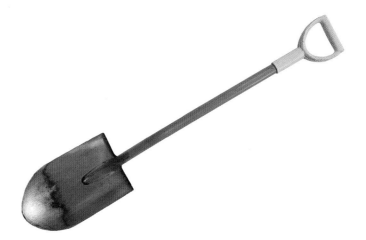

We see and use simple machines every day.

What simple machines can you find at the playground?

Answer Key

Page 5   **What else uses an inclined plane?** The slide, the escalator, and the ladder all use inclined planes.

Page 7   **How many inclined planes can you find at this water park?** There are four inclined planes in this water park.

Page 9   **Which of these items are wedges?** The scissors, knife, and nail are all wedges.

Page 11   **What other objects are screws?** The light bulb, bottle cap, and screw are all types of screws.

Page 13   **What kinds of wheels and axles do you see in this picture?** The bicycle, skateboard, scooter, and rollerblades all use wheels and axles.

Page 15   **What pulleys do you see at work in this picture?** Sailboats have ropes. The ropes are a kind of pulley. They raise and lower the sails.

Page 17   **Can you identify the lever and fulcrum in this picture?** The lever is the handle of the hammer. The fulcrum is the top of the hammer. When you apply force, the lever lifts the nail.

Page 19   **Which of these gardening tools are levers?** The shovel and hedge clippers are both types of levers.

Glossary

circular (SUR-kyuh-luhr) Circular means something moves in a circle or spiral. Screws move in a circular motion.

effort (EF-urft) Effort is the force used to move a load. When you push down on a lever, you are applying effort.

force (FORS) Force is strength or power. Force is used on a lever.

fulcrum (FUL-kruhm) A fulcrum is the point on which a lever rests or turns. A seesaw balances on a fulcrum.

gravity (GRAV-i-tee) Gravity is the force that pulls things toward the center of the Earth and keeps them from floating away. Gravity makes moving things down an inclined plane easy.

lever (LEV-ur) A lever is a bar that rests on a fulcrum and is used to lift something. We use a lever to lift heavy objects.

pulley (PUL-ee) A pulley is a wheel with a groove in it for a rope or chain. A pulley is used to lift heavy objects, such as on a crane.

screw (SKROO) A screw is a simple machine that is similar to an inclined plane but with a spiral, or twist. A light bulb is an example of a screw.

wedge (WEJ) A wedge is a piece of material that is slanted and thick on one end and thin on the other. A wood axe is an example of a wedge.

To Learn More

Books

LaMachia, Dawn. *Wheels and Axles at Work*. New York, NY: Enslow Publishing, 2016.

Rice, Dona Herweck. *Good Work: Simple Tools*. Huntington Beach, CA: Teacher Created Materials, 2016.

Schuh, Mari C. *Playing a Game: Inclined Plane vs. Lever*. Minneapolis, MN: Lerner Publications, 2016.

Web Sites

Visit our Web site for links about simple machines:
childsworld.com/links

Note to Parents, Teachers, and Librarians: We routinely verify our Web links to make sure they are safe and active sites. So encourage your readers to check them out!